Diane the Turtle

and Her New Found Joy

Written by Jim and Brad Tonner
Illustrated by Brad Tonner

ISBN: 0997412534
ISBN-13: 978-0997412536
Library of Congress Control Number: 2016918560
Printed: North Charleston, South Carolina

This book is dedicated to
Lisa Showalter Hopkins

One of Diane the Turtle's
best friends. Whose joy,
enthusiasm and courage
will never be forgotten.
She will continue to
inspire all who were
fortunate enough to
have known her.

TO

LiLi AND BEN

All THE BEST

Jim AND BRAD

TONNER

AND of COURSE

DIANE

THE TURTLE

Diane the Turtle

and Her New Found Joy

Written by Jim and Brad Tonner
Illustrated by Brad Tonner

BRAD TONNER

People travel from all over
the world to come to a gift shop
in the small town of
Bristol, New Hampshire.

They come from near and far.
Friends like Wayne walk to the store.

Some need Harold the Crossing Guard
to help them cross the street.

Some drive and some fly.

BRAD TONNER

Others come on motorcycles,
like Joann, Walter, Zelia and Paul.

What are all these people
coming to see?

They are coming to see Diane the Turtle!
She has lived with twin brothers
Jim and Brad Tonner since 1968.

Her visitors are all ages.

She has been visited by
cats, dogs, rabbits, parrots and
turtles. Even a fish has come to
visit her!

One day her friend Suzanne
stopped by and surprised her
with a strawberry.

We found something out that day.
Diane loves strawberries!

Avery visits Diane every day after school.
One day she brought her cat to meet Diane.

Ernie, an editor from a famous newspaper,
visited Diane one day.

Teacher Jen stopped by on a cold
winters day to see Diane with
Dominic, Teagan, Ellie, CJ, Joseph,
Andrew, William, Aubrey, Olivia, Juniper,
Fiona, Kendall, Olive, Alden, Kaliegh and
teacher Meghan.

An actor visited Diane.

One day a violinist surprised
Diane with a visit.

A nurse named Cynthia
came by.

Even a fire chief came by
to say hello.

She has been visited by a policeman.

And when the circus came to town
the clown visited.

Dawn, a newspaper reporter,
interviewed Diane.

A famous TV show came and
interviewed Diane. She was the star
of the show.

What has Diane the Turtle found with
all these wonderful people visiting her?

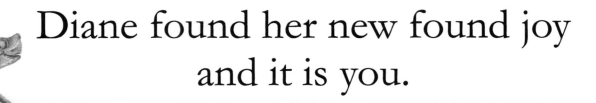

Diane found her new found joy and it is you.

Here is where to put your picture if you have had one taken with Diane the Turtle. You can also draw a picture of Diane the Turtle.

Diane the Turtle
Thanks everyone for joining in her fun.

Did you have your picture taken with Diane the Turtle?
See if you can find yourself in the following pages.

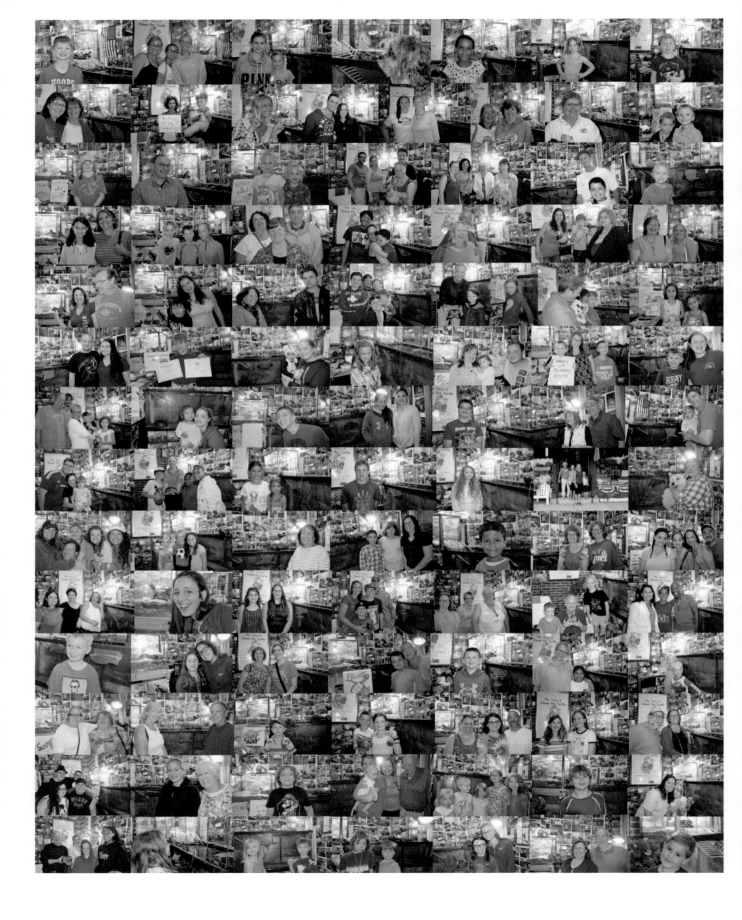

Made in the USA
Charleston, SC
11 December 2016